www.kiltiris.com

About us
propos de nous
cerca de nosotros

Francklin Pierre

ISBN 978-0-557-07808-0

About us

Special thanks

To all of those people who participated to realization

of this publication, specially:

Francesca Palli (Switzerland)

Michèle Trévien (France)

Paula Salomon (Argentina)

I dedicate this work to the "College Roger A. Anglade", my

former secondary school.

And to the memory of my grand father and my grand mother:

Saint Louis Pierre and Osanna Lestin

Table of Contents /Table des matières/Contenidos

INTRODUCTION

Very deep in my heart I consider myself as a citizen of the world. I cannot think about people outside the context of a universal body. The idea of a Carrefour where every essential aspect of culture would meet is an ideal I dearly like to see materialized.

I wondered whether somebody is about thinking or dreaming same as I do. Hence, I decided more recently to lunch a survey over the web system seeking to verify whether other people, of all ages, living in different regions of our planet, would be attracted by the idea of an intercultural exchange or dialogue.

As I just started to transform this idea into an outreaching project, I imagined eight short questions which would permit to some people to say: who they are, where they from, where they are, what they are frightened of, what's their wish for the world, what they love and pay attention to, what is positive about their own culture, which foreign people they may come about to think of and why. Yet I am very glad of the primary outcome of my effort. The best of the world is responding.

Here I am sharing with you all a few sessions of my encounter with the world on line.

NICEA (DANEMARK)

- What is your name?

- My name is Nicea

- Your place of birth?

- I was born in *Niböl*, at the border between Denmark and Germany.

- Are you living in your country of birth? And if not why did you choose to live where you are?

- I don't live in Denmark anymore; I'm currently living in Sweden. I came here to study, and I don't know whether I will return to live in Denmark later, I think I would rather live in Africa or somewhere else in the world.

- What are you and your closer friends frightened of, in the world?

- I think we're scared of the current world order, where America has unlimited power and exploits the rest of the world, and ignores international law and starts wars for no reason.

- In one word what is your wish for the world?

-    Peace.

-    Say a positive thing you like or you pay a little attention to, in the world!

-    Human rights, nature and humanity.

-    If you would like to present or talk about something of positive about the culture of your country of birth, the town or the community where you are living, what could it be?

-    Stockholm is a beautiful place; build on islands with lots of water and lots of parks. Now in summer, the sun hardly sets and we have long and light nights. This also makes people happy and in summer everybody smiles and is friendly. Everybody goes to the parks for picnics or parties, and that's fun!

-    Tell us about a foreign country that, you have not visited yet, but which for a reason or other, comes in your mind sometimes or often. And what are your wishes for this country's population?

-    There are so many places I would like to go: I would love to go to India, because I believe that it is a very spiritual place full of variety. I wish the people in India could teach the rest of the world about spirituality and life. I would also like to go to Jamaica; I imagine that it is really relaxed and easy. Keep up the spirit, Jamaica! I'm also a big fan of Africa, and I would like to go to places like Malawi, South Africa and Mali. I hope that the African countries can find their own way to find solutions to problems.

EXTRA

Good luck with your book, Nicea.

NAT SCANDINAVIAN (SWITZERLAND)

- What is your name?

- Nat

- Your place of birth?

- Locarno

- Are you living in your country of birth? And if not why did you choose to live where you are?

- Yes, I am living in my country of birth

- What are you and your closer friends frightened of, in the world?

- Of the fact to don't find a job, to loose important person in your life.

- In one word, what is your wish for the world?

- Live a beautiful life

- Say a positive thing you like or you pay a little attention to, in the world!

- My girlfriend, my family, my friends, Magic the Gathering.

- If you would like to present or talk about something of positive about the culture of your country of birth, the town, or the community where you are living, what could it be?

- I don't know.

- Tell us about a foreign country that you have not visited yet, but which for a reason or other, comes in your mind sometimes or often. And what are your wishes for this country's population?

- I love country like Tunisia, but I have already visited it. Hope people could live better and not destroy their nature.

NICOLA (SWITZERLAND)

- What is your name?

- Nicola

- Your place of birth?

- Locarno, Switzerland

- Are you living in your country of birth? And if not why did you choose to live where you are?

- I live in my country of birth.

- What are you and your closer friends frightened of, in the world?

- People who kill animal without a reason.

- In one word, what is your wish for the world?

- That aliens attack the earth, so people in earth stand united against the unknown enemy

- Say a positive thing you like or you pay a little attention to, in the world!

- Music

- If you would like to present or talk about something of positive about the culture of your country of birth, the town, or the community where you are living, what could it be?

- Switzerland always remains neutral, in every war...

- Tell us about a foreign country that you have not visited yet, but which for a reason or other, comes in your mind sometimes or often. And what are your wishes for this country's population?

- I would like to visit the U.S.A. especially the west coast, California, and Miami... I wish that American people become less conservative and more open to new ideas...

ANA MARIA (SWITZERLAND)

- What is your name?

- Annamaria

- Your place of birth?

- Switzerland

- Are you living in your country of birth? And if not why did you choose to live where you are?

- Yes, I am

- What are you and your closer friends frightened of, in the world?

- War, environment catastrophes, luck of justice.

- In one word, what is your wish for the world?

- Peace.

- Say a positive thing you like or you pay a little attention to, in the world!

- Differences between the people.

- If you would like to present or talk about something of positive about the culture of your country of birth, the town or the community where you are living, what could it be?

- It's a very quiet and safe place to live.

- Tell us about a foreign country that you have not visited yet, but which for a reason or other, comes in your mind sometimes or often. And what are your wishes for this country's population?

- In fact, I think about several countries, the most known, that have a difficult situation social, political, economical, and obviously my wish for these people is a better situation, an improvement.

DIDAR (TURQUEY)

- What is your name?

- Didar

- Your place of birth?

- Gaziantep, Turkey.

- Are you living in your country of birth? And if not why did you choose to live where you are?

- I don't live in my country of birth because when I was child my parents have moved from Turkey to Switzerland because of the politic conflict between Turkish and Kurdish people.

- What are you and your closer friends frightened of, in the world?

- We are frightened of the war and the advancement of the multination.

- In one word, what is your wish for the world?

- Peace

- Say a positive thing you like or you pay a little attention to, in the world!

- Friendship

- If you would like to present or talk about something of positive about the culture of your country of birth, the town, or the community where you are living, what could it be?

- The chocolate is good... but also the town is very peaceful. The people are a bit conservative but very open to another people of another country.

- Tell us about a foreign country that you have not visited yet, but which for a reason or other, comes in your mind sometimes or often. And what are your wishes for this country's population?

- I wish to visit INDIA because the Indian are very peaceful And quiet people.... also the culture is very interesting. My wishes for the people are that the people of the all world live in peace and never make war... and I wish that the people become more helpful.

KATRIN (SWITZERLAND)

My name is Katrin Schneider and I was born in Muralto, a little town in Ticino Switzerland. Now I live in Ascona which is another little village in Ticino about ten minutes time from Murarlto.

What I'm frightened of is that nature will finally rebel against us, for all the harm that we have done to her in the last years. I'm worried about the future because I fear that my children might get into a seriously troubled world. I'm also worried about the men's ambition for money and power because we might loose all the beautiful things that make the world worth living in.

In one word, what I wish is for the world is: tolerance!! And if I had to say something positive about my culture or my country, I would say that it is a fee democratic country. Generally people are friendly and cooperative. Sadly there are also people that are so used to this wealthy life that they don't think about poor countries.

Since I'm very little I have been wishing to go to Cuba. I think that it is a strong and amazing country. I find it inspiring and i really would like to explore it, to meet the people and learn the culture and the music. To the people I would like to say that they should try to do their best without judging the others. Help others if you can just because it's beautiful to help, not because you expect something back.

JAN (SWITZERLAND)

My name is Jan; I was born in Locarno, Switzerland. Yes I live in my country, and I think that I'll stay in Switzerland...

What my friends and I are frightened of is that my country becomes poor. My wish for the world is: peace, equality for all the people and I hope that one day all people will live together like they were brothers the nature, which we should protect mountains, fresh air, beautiful lakes, good cheese.

I'd like to visit some of the Caribbean countries, for example Jamaica, panama, Cuba and why not also Haiti... and many other countries. Good luck for life, Jan

MARCO (SWITZERLAND)

- What is your name?

- My name is Marco Simona

- Your place of birth?

- I was born in Locarno

- Are you living in your country of birth? And if not why did you choose to live where you are?

- Yes, I'm living near it, in a little village called Arcegno.

- What are you and your closer friends are frightened of, in the world?

- The destruction of the forests, but also maybe a third world war for the natural sources like water.

- In one word, what is your wish for the world?

- I think that the most important thing is the respect: we have to respect nature, the other people also if they're different, and we have to be tolerant.

- Say a positive thing you like or you pay a little attention to, in the world!

- Music, I love music very much and I think that it can unit all the peoples of the world.

- If you would like to present or talk about something of positive about the culture of your country of birth, the town, or the community where you are living, what could it be?

- Switzerland is a very safe place, where there isn't so much poverty. There are three different cultures and it's a bit difficult to find a common point. I think that my part of Switzerland is a very hospital place.

- Tell us about a foreign country that you have not visited yet, but which for a reason or other, comes in your mind sometimes or often. And what are your wishes for this country's population?

- I'd like to visit Japan, because I like very much the culture, but I'd like that Japanese people would find again the spirituality and the respect of nature they had in the past.

UJAGER (PAKISTAN)

My name is Farhan Sabir Ujager, I was born in Mardan, Pakistan. I'm living in my home land and I would like to live in the same Country; reasons: first I love my country and secondly I want to be part in my country's progress.

I m frightened of nothing except God and myself. What I wish for the world is: Peace, to stop sectarian, religious extremism. Things I like and pay attention to is: Family and Social values. I never visited any country; I would like that people from the united Sate of America try to know other people outside of U.S.A.

LUKE (USA)

My name is Luke Lieberman; I was born in New York, USA. I am living in America, there is no other place I could so readily follow my dream of becoming a filmmaker and storyteller - I have moved to Los Angeles on the West coast.

I don't think most of my friends are frightened of anything in particular really. Personally my greatest concern is that my hometown of New York, which is physically very small, will be destroyed in an act of terrorism, it is truly the greatest city in the world, and it bother that it is such a target.

My wish for the world in one world is: Peace.

I am encouraged to see formerly third world nations like China and India - which have so many of the worlds poor begin to get their economies on the right track

I love New York - there is no place I feel more at home, and all of the world's cultures, Christian, Jewish, Muslim, Chinese, Italian, Korean, Indian, Japanese, English, African etc are all on top of one another, mixed together - it gives the place a lot of flavor, it is like all the cultures of the world have come to share a thirty Square mile island and they do so peacefully, without factional violence or hostility. I hope to visit both India and china but have not gotten there yet. They are ancient cultures and massive countries and I am certain there will be many things I see there that I have never seen before.

THEOBALD BANDA (ZANBIA)

My name is Theobald Banda. I was born in Kitwe, in the Copperbelt, Zambia. I am living in my country of birth. My friends and I, We are not frightened by anything.

My wish for the world is: To be at peace and unity. Today one thing I pay attention to is the welfare of the children and the youths that their voices be head, concerning their rights.

If I want to talk about something of positive in my country, it could be about the hospitality and love of my people.

I always think of the Middle-East, these people need peace and it's only through those countries that are at peace to enforce it on them too. And I think and trust that through this we all going to benefit.

TERENZIA (TOGO)

My name is Chantal Tchotcho Dossou Adotevi. Place of birth: Loma, Togo; I am living in my country of birth.

What frightens me more is the actual belief of the world in war because we are young and without peace and stability of our countries and governments we don't have any future to have hope in. I am also afraid of all the evils and lies in this world today you don't know who to believe and what to do. Life has no meaning for me in this world now apart from you religious belief.

My wish for the world in one world is: Harmony.

What I like is all that forms the nature including human's good beings. What I pay a little attention to is violence, pursuit of illegal money.

What I can say about Loma is that it used to be a very wonderful place where live is very easy with nice people where security was our every day song and where with a little money or effort you can do a great thing. But all these have reduced today. About the culture I can say hat it is a place where every nationality finds a way because we have a mixed cultural that resembles a lot in this world especially in Africa.

I would like to visit South Africa one day, because of what they have endured. They suffered for all the blacks and we have to be in one though with them. I would like that they forget all the souvenirs of that time of tears and see the new smile on their faces. To them I want to say make a good use of your freedom and forget the past better things are ahead of us. God bless you and god blesses Africa.

CHRISTINE (CANADA)

My name is Christine McPhail; I was born in Canada Yes I still live in Canada. Canada is close to the United States and is very prosperous for still a very young country.

My friends and I are frightened of war. Canada is much younger than many countries in the world. We made our way into the world through World War 1 and World War 2 and like other countries lost many people but we have less experience making us feel unsafe. We fear terrorism because we are not prepared for another 911 like in the U.S.A. we; as a country do not believe in terrorism.

My wish for the world is: Freedom. I love the Olympics and how we all come together it's amazing how we can once every year come together as one instead of being separate.

I would talk about the arts of dance in Canada we have so many talented companies and theatre companies that all around are amazing! The N.A.C. theatre is a beautiful place near the parliament buildings in Ottawa and the arts are performed here to remind everyone of how beautiful our life really is and how fortunate we are.

I often think of Africa, Yugoslavia and some other poor countries. I think about them because I believe richer countries like the United States England and Canada could help but we don't enough. My wish for these people is for them to have the right to follow their dreams and live the way they want to live not the way other countries are telling them they have to live. If we could give these workers and people that extra few cents they would be able to go to school, eat, and be prosperous. World Vision a child's sponsor program in Canada is doing they're best but we need support from others so please help today!

EXTRA

Let's come together in peace and put all the wars and problems behind us that we had in the past. Come forth as ONE and let people have their right to their dreams and their future.

Thanks,

Christine McPhail

ESTHER (UKRAINE)

- What is your name?

- My name is Esther Montvai.

- Your Place of birth?

- I was born in Kiev, Ukraine (Soviet Union).

- Are you living in your country of birth? And if not why did you choose to live where you are?

- Now, I'm living in Hungary, because my parents came here to live when I was very young. "I was born in Kiev because my mother had been studying here economics as change student."

- What are you and your closer friends frightened of, in the world?

- My friends and I are frightened of war, homelessness, unhappiness.

- In one word, what is your wish for the world?

- My wish for the world is peace and happiness.

- Say a positive thing you like or you pay a little attention to, in the world!

- What I like and pay attention to is: different supporting initiatives, and associating like TIG for example.

- If you would like to present or talk about something of positive about the culture of your country of birth, the town, or the community where you are living, what could it be?

- In my community what I appreciate is the friendship of people, and that they love their country.

- Tell us about a foreign country that you have not visited yet, but which for a reason or other, comes in your mind sometimes or often. And what are your wishes for this country's population?

- Sweden, Norway, Japan. I wish these people will more positive, optimistic, and open to the world and other people, if we could trust in each other. Trust is very important in connecting people

FARHAN (PAKISTAN)

- What is your name?

- My name is Farhan Saghar Randhawa.

- Your place of birth?

- Are you living in your country of birth? And if not why did you choose to live where you are?

- I am living in my country of birth. I am living in Faisalabad.

- What are you and your closer friends frightened of, in the world?

- Dishonest and liars scared me. And my closest friend, as I know he is frightened of deep water.

- In one word, what is your wish for the world?

- Love

- Say a positive thing you like or you pay a little attention to, in the world!

- My wife is so precious to me and all my attention is for her.

- If you would like to present or talk about something of positive about the culture of your country of birth, the town or the community where you are living, what could it be?

- The culture and traditions of my beloved Pakistan are great. And the most attractive thing from my culture is to love every one with out any reward. The purity of the loving people is admirable.

- Tell us about a foreign country, that you have not visited yet, but which for a reason or other, comes in your mind sometimes or often. And what are your wishes for this country's population?

- I would love to Visit Africa. I want to see the African way of living.

EXTRA: So that's all you need to know I think. Best wishes, Farhan S. Randhawa

CORMELIUS (SIERA LEONE)

My name is Cornelius Deveaux. I was born in Freetown, in Sierra Leone and I still live there. My friends and I are frightened of war, famine, hunger, non curable diseases.

My wish for the world and specially my community is peace, good governance and access to information technology.

MARTIN KIMANI (KENYA)

- What is your name?

- Martin Mbugua Kimani

- Your place of birth?

- Kakamega town, western province-Kenya

- Are you living in your country of birth? And if not why did you choose to live where you are?

- Yes

- What are you and your closer friends frightened of, in the world?

- Joblessness and poverty

- In one word, what is your wish for the world?

- Eradicate Poverty

- Say a positive thing you like or you pay a little attention to, in the world!

- Service to humanity is service to God

- If you would like to present or talk about something of positive about the culture of your country of birth, the town or the community where you are living, what could it be?

- Means of creative self employment to youth in my District.

- Tell us about a foreign country, that you have not visited yet, but which for a reason or other, comes in your mind sometimes or often. And what are your wishes for this country's population?

- It is France, I like there language though I can not express myself frequently. There Culture is fantastic

KATHARINE (USA)

- What is your name?

- Katharine Chu

- Your place of birth?

- Lewisville, Texas, USA

- Are you living in your country of birth? And if not why did you choose to live where you are?

- Yes

- What are you and your closer friends frightened of, in the world?

- Ignorance, I'm afraid that people one day won't be able to do what is right because they won't know, or won't care to know.

- In one word, what is your wish for the world?

- I would wish happiness for the world. I hope that everyone in the world is able to find a place in society and find happiness there. I'm so glad that there are different people in the world. I rarely ever think about it, but I'm glad that there are people with different beliefs that can challenge my beliefs and that I can learn from.

- Say a positive thing you like or you pay a little attention to, in the world!

- I love the close bonding that Texas has. Most people here are like one big family. When new neighbors move in, we usually hold a block party and a "BBQ" where everyone in the town comes out to meet the new neighbors. The fire and police department also come out just so the kids can ride in the fire truck and police cars for fun.

- Tell us about a foreign country, that you have not visited yet, but which for a reason or other, comes in your mind sometimes or often. And what are your wishes for this country's population?

- South Africa. I have several friends from S. Africa and there have been so many dramatic changes in their country's past that have permanently shaped so many of their citizens. South Africa is a country with such a distinctive history, and I honestly believe that the dramatic changes that have occurred there truly show the good and the bad, the strengths and the weaknesses of human nature.

AGUOGIEYIN IGUMAH (NIGERIA)

- What is your name?

- Aguogieyin Igumah Osazuwa

- Your place of birth?

- Oza-nogogo agbor Nigeria

- Are you living in your country of birth? And if not why did you choose to live where you are?

- Yes

- What are you and your closer friends frightened of, in the world?

44

- HIV /aids, war.

- In one word, what is your wish for the world?

- Peace

- Say a positive thing you like or you pay a little attention to, in the world!

- Campaigns to eradicate poverty and HIV aids

- If you would like to present or talk about something of positive about the culture of your country of birth, the town, or the community where you are living, what could it be?

- Dress and food

- Tell us about a foreign country, that you have not visited yet, but which for a reason or other, comes in your mind sometimes or often. And what are your wishes for this country's population?

- Britain, because of their openness in assisting underdeveloped countries

RAYMOND (GHANA)

My name is Raymond Selorm Mamattah. Place of birth: Dodi-akum, Volta region, in Ghana. I am living in my country of birth at the moment.

What is my most fear as well as my friends in the world is where my soul goes after I die. What do I gain, should I all of a sudden fall down and never to rise again? Where else is my life. Those who believe in life after death will appreciate this much more.

My wish for the world is "PEACE" and one thing I pay attention to in the world is that, I believe with God by our side, things will be a bit better for us.

My country is noted for the peace it enjoins in the sub-region. This "I believe" is possible because, Ghana is full of people who, despite all odds, are fully aware that, without peace in the country, we have no where else to go. Other culture of my town folks or Ghanaians so to say is respect for the elderly, though not as good as it used to be, as we are always told by the elderly in the society. Ghanaians give respect to the elderly in the society. Ghanaians are also noted for the reverence they give to their parents.

What is more interesting is the extended family system which we so much enjoy. Uncles and aunts could easily take care of their nephews and nieces, which, of course as we see in movies and read in books are not applicable to other parts of the world.

I use to think of Canada, Canada is a country that I would wish to visit. I head it is a country that is now building up. I heard it is full of all races. I would like to visit there because I am made to understand racism is not there and life is a bit okay. To the people of Canada, continue being good to your fellow man, irrespective of the color and language for we are all one.

Even the chariot is prepared for battle; success is in the hands of the lord!

EMMANUEL (NIGERIA)

I had the opportunity to ask questions to some people directly. And Emanuel is one of them. Read what has been said, bellow.

-   Francklin Pierre: What is your name?

-   Olaoye olusoji Emmanuel: My name is Olaoye olusoji Emmanuel.

-   Francklin Pierre: Your place of birth?

-   Olaoye olusoji Emmanuel: Lagos, Nigeria

- Francklin Pierre: Are you living in your country of birth?

- Olaoye olusoji Emmanuel: yes

- Francklin Pierre: What are you and your closer friends frightened of, in the world?

- Olaoye olusoji Emmanuel: War

- Francklin Pierre: You have some words that you would like to say about it?

- Olaoye Olusoji Emmanuel: YES

- Francklin Pierre: What exactly?

- Olaoye olusoji Emmanuel: campaign for absolute PEACE in the WORLD through Media

- Francklin Pierre: In one word, what is your wish for the world?

- Olaoye olusoji Emmanuel: PEACE

- Francklin Pierre: good!

- Francklin Pierre: Say a positive thing you like or you pay a little attention to, in the world!

- Olaoye Olusoji Emmanuel: Olaoye shoji is founder of Media for Ethnic Equality (MEE), an organization that is involved in organizing seminars, musical concerts, events, rallies etc, to motivate and inspire youths to be a potential life changer, in other for them to affect someone's life positively. To campaign against HIV/AIDS disease by creating awareness and publicity that AIDS IS REAL. And finally to campaign for absolute PEACE in the WORLD through Media

- Francklin Pierre: It could be something else?

- Olaoye olusoji Emmanuel: Friendship, group and movement

- Francklin Pierre: you like when people are grouping for friendship movement?

- Olaoye olusoji Emmanuel: YES

- Francklin Pierre: If you would like to present or talk about something of positive about the culture of your country of birth, the town, the community where you are living, what could it be?

- Olaoye Olusoji Emmanuel: music and dance

- FRANCKLIN: Tell us about a foreign country, that you have not visited yet, but which for a reason or other, comes in your mind sometimes or often.

- Olaoye Olusoji Emmanuel: Malta

- FRANCKLIN: What are your wishes and specials words for the population of Malta?

- Olaoye Olusoji Emmanuel: I hope they like to make friend with people, love people and live with them with respect.

SIHAM (UNITED ARAB EMIRAT)

- What is your name?

- Siham Al Najmi

- Your place of birth?

- Dubai, UAE

- Are you living in your country of birth? And if not why did you choose to live where you are?

- Yes I am living in the country I was born in.

What are you and your closer friends frightened of, in the world?

- I don't know about my friends, but being a Muslim, I have been taught to fear only Allah (God). Of course many of us have our fears in life but again we have to distinguish between fears and worries. For me, I go through life's difficulties by the guidance of faith and trust in Allah and my family. My philosophy in life is: do your best and leave the rest on Allah. Live the present day and tomorrow is another day. As for being worry, I came to realize that worrying is acting childish about various situations that a person is forced to deal with.

- In one word, what is your wish for the world?

- Coexistence

- Say a positive thing you like or you pay a little attention to, in the world!

- Humanity and similarity, I think in times of crisis we forget our biases and differences and remember that no matter how different we are, we still are humans breathing the same air. Unfortunately, we are remembered of that only in times of crises.

- If you would like to present or talk about something of positive about the culture of your country of birth, the town, or the community where you are living, what could it be?

- The value of family and collectivism. Arab countries are more described as living in a collective society as compared to other countries. Families and parents are very important in building up a community, in my opinion. Most individuals are affected by their childhood and to a great extent, consciously or unconsciously, we are affected by the way we have been raised. Thus, focusing on building a healthy family is a good way to nourish the builders of the future. In UAE, family is an important element of their culture.

- Tell us about a foreign country, that you have not visited yet, but which for a reason or other, comes in your mind sometimes or often. And what are your wishes for this country's population?

- Well, I always struggled to know where I belong and from where am I. I'm a person who doesn't have a passport but a document that proves I'm a Palestinian. Both my parents were born in Palestine in 1945 and migrated to Lebanon after the 1948 war with Israel. They lived in Lebanon for almost 30 years, and had their two first kids there. However, in 1980 they migrated again away from the war in Lebanon to live in UAE, Dubai. As I mentioned earlier, Dubai is my place of birth and till this day I live here. As for my ancestors from my mother's side, they are from turkey and Moroccans from my father's side. After loads of thinking, I have come to realize that it doesn't matter at all from where I am. See, my philosophy in life is that Allah almighty created earth without dividing it into different countries and set boundaries to them and I think there is a reason for that. Unfortunately, these boundaries are not only physical but in our subconscious mind they are becoming social ones too. As soon as you mention your nationality to any one there is an image photographed in the other person's mind. For me, I'd rather belong to a cause or a belief rather than a piece of land. Come to think about all counties are a pieces of lands given different names.

EXTRA

Thank you for your time and efforts and I wish you all the best in writing and publishing your book. If you need assistance, then please don't hesitate to ask for it. I hope I answered your questions as intended. One more thing, please don't associate what I have written to being an Arab or Muslim, my opinions reflect only myself. It is true that I am greatly inspired by the belief I have chosen for myself and that is ISLAM but also I am only a human being characterized as many are for being imperfect and subject to corruption. And my religion is not subject to that. Unfortunately, as it has been circulated in many media outlets, Islam is been synonymous to terrorism and when people say that, I know that they don't know anything about Islam because I know for sure they wouldn't say that if they have read the Holy Quran. Also I'm not trying to say that my religion is the only true religion and I'm right and everybody else is wrong. The point I'm trying to illustrate is, I'm always welcome to people's opinions, I do not mind if people disagree about some aspects in Islam but I totally get offended when people disrespect my religion. For instance by saying, "Islam is the religion of terrorism and oppression."

God bless you, Siham

AMATE (NIGERIA)

- What is your name?

- My name is Amire Ademola

- Your place of birth?

- Lagos State, Nigeria

- Are you living in your country of birth? And if not why did you choose to live where you are?

- Yes, I am living in the country of my birth

- What are you and your closer friends frightened of, in the world?

- Nothing but with God & effort of Mankind all thing works well and perfect.

- In one word, what is your wish for the world?

- Peace

- Say a positive thing you like or you pay a little attention to, in the world!

- Some people are fighting for one World bounded with Love.

- If you would like to present or talk about something of positive about the culture of your country of birth, the town, or the community where you are living, what could it be?

- Good and harmony

- Tell us about a foreign country, that you have not visited yet, but which for a reason or other, comes in your mind sometimes or often. And what are your wishes for this country's population?

- Canada. Just the best place to have sound education, a comfortable living. Wish to study & work there soonest. Canada is a beautiful country in it wildness and vastness. I am looking forward for a loving and caring person to make my dream a reality. I wish everybody best of things in Life and peace and love abound us all.

AKUNNE (NIGERIA)

- What is your name?

- Akunne Chike Mario

- Your place of birth?

- Lagos Nigeria

- Are you living in your country of birth? And if not why did you choose to live where you are?

- Yes

- What are you and your closer friends frightened of, in the world?

- Lack of opportunity to express ourselves because of biting poverty and neglect of the youth by our government.

- In one word, what is your wish for the world?

- Love

- Say a positive thing you like or you pay a little attention to, in the world!

- Global peace and international security founded on genuine love and care for humanity.

- If you would like to present or talk about something of positive about the culture of your country of birth, the town, or the community where you are living, what could it be?

- Culture as an instrument of nation building in the face of modernity.

- Tell us about a foreign country, that you have not visited yet, but which for a reason or other, comes in your mind sometimes or often. And what are your wishes for this country's population?

- United States of America... that the human race is just one, not minding color or geographical location.

ANDY RYAN (ENGLAND)

- What is your name?

- Andy Ryan.

- Your place of birth?

- Windsor, England

- Are you living in your country of birth? And if not why did you choose to live where you are?

- Yes

- What are you and your closer friends frightened of, in the world?

- Religious fundamentalism and the power it has.

- In one word, what is your wish for the world?

- Smiles

- Say a positive thing you like or you pay a little attention to, in the world!

- The courage and the heart I see exhibited in many who experience great suffering.

- If you would like to present or talk about something of positive about the culture of your country of birth, the town, or the community where you are living, what could it be?

- England - the land of the spirit of fair play.

- Tell us about a foreign country, that you have not visited yet, but which for a reason or other, comes in your mind sometimes or often. And what are your wishes for this country's population?

- Zimbabwe. I lived there a brief time and I can't describe the anger and the sadness I feel when I see this beautiful country being torn apart by one man's thirst for power.

ANOUK (NETHERLAND)

My name is Anouk Vos and I was born in Groningen, The Netherlands. At the moment I am living in my country of birth.

I can say that I am not frightened by anything in this world in particular, since as an adolescent I sometimes feel like the world is mine and I am about to conquer it. Fear is what makes people hold back from acting and therefore stopping them from changing the world into a better place. Like Wilson said; the only thing to fear is fear itself.

My wish for this world is climate control, sustainable development and redistribution of wealth. In one word I would say this would mean comfort for everybody in the world, since peace alone does not bring about a good life. There are more threats in this world then just from the outside of the people that surround us.

I pay attention to other people in that way that I listen to other people and do anything in my power to put a smile on their faces.

The most positive thing I can mention about my country or my culture I would say that that is the tolerance of our people. I myself and my friends do not judge a book on its cover. We enjoy other cultures and interact with them in stead of avoiding them. We respect other people and become better people by learning and adopting other cultures in our own way of life.

I myself have never visited Georgia, but sometimes I think about this country and the challenges it has to overcome. I think about their international position and their strategic position between East en West and north and South. Are the Georgian people ready to build a bridge between all of their neighboring countries? Can they become an example of tolerance and freedom in a messy area between so many cultures and religions, between Capitalism and Communism? Georgia is the hometown of the first Homo sapiens and therefore it would be great if they could stabilize and evolve into a great free country in order to bring its Homo sapiens into a perfect resting place. So that not only in a historical way but also in utopian way Georgia could be the place that not only brought about the human being but perhaps also humanity.

SIMBARASHE NHLEMA (ZIMBABWE)

- What is your name?

- Simbarashe Nhlema.

- Your place of birth?

- Chinhoyi, Zimbabwe

- Are you living in your country of birth? And if not why did you choose to live where you are?

- Yes.

- What are you and your closer friends frightened of, in the world?

- A Possible World War 3

- In one word, what is your wish for the world?

- Peace.

- Say a positive thing you like or you pay a little attention to, in the world!

- Development

- If you would like to present or talk about something of positive about the culture of your country of birth, the town, or the community where you are living, what could it be?

- My people really respect their culture; we are people who believe in our tradition, although we believe in the bible as well

- Tell us about a foreign country, that you have not visited yet, but which for a reason or other, comes in your mind sometimes or often. And what are your wishes for this country's population?

- China - I really respect the Chinese because they are a people with culture. There is no cultural decadence in China. I really adore them.

EXTRA:

I hope I have answered you adequately. I also would like to ask the same to you.

MOHAMMED SAAED (IRAQ)

- What is your name?

- Mohammed Saaed

- Your place of birth?

- Baghdad, Iraq.

- Are you living in your country of birth? And if not why did you choose to live where you are?

- Yes

- What are you and your closer friends frightened of, in the world?

- Some of my close friends may differ with me but as far as I'm concerned, ignorance, poverty and lack of freedom.

- In one word, what is your wish for the world?

- Justice

- Say a positive thing you like or which you pay a little attention to, in the world!

- It relieves me to see a good number of people willing to help people of other countries.

- If you would like to present or talk about something of positive about the culture of your country of birth or the town, the community where you are living, what it could be?

- It would certainly be about the ceremonies that we have every year to remember Al Imam Al Husayn, I think the story of Al Husayn has many valuable lessons that we can learn, and it's a story about not submitting to oppression. There's no way I can tell you about it so if you're interested visit "www.ashura.com"

- Tell us about a foreign country, that you have not visited yet, but which for a reason or other, comes in your mind sometimes or often. And what are your wishes for this country's population?

- The United States of America. America saved us from Saddam and made our first direct free elections possible. I know this is a controversial topic but this is the way I feel it. I want to tell the people there, that the American soldiers in my country are fighting for a noble cause and I appreciate what they're doing and thank you so much.

ANTONY SIMBOWO (KENYA)

- What is your name?

- Antony Simbowo.

- Your place of birth?

- Kenya

- Are you living in your country of birth? And if not why did you choose to live where you are?

- Yes.

- What are you and your closer friends frightened of, in the world?

- Nothing

- In one word, what is your wish for the world?

- Justice

- Say a positive thing you like or you pay a little attention to, in the world!

- The Equality for all fighting.

- If you would like to present or talk about something of positive about the culture of your country of birth, the town, or the community where you are living, what could it be?

- Hard work and culture.

- Tell us about a foreign country, that you have not visited yet, but which for a reason or other, comes in your mind sometimes or often. And what are your wishes for this country's population?

- Mongolia-has plenty of horses, livestock and a fine traditional lifestyle. Let them invest on education and development infrastructure even as they also maintain their cultural identity, which they should never dilute.

PHYLLIS (HONG KONG)

- I am Phyllis from Hong Kong, but I live in Sydney, Australia most of the time, due to the fact that I attend high school there. I and my closer friends are frightened of only fear itself. We fear 'fear' because it is a feeling that we can't be immune from.

I wish one day, everyone would be able to travel to one another's country without having any barriers and be able to embrace each other's cultures and beliefs.

If I would like to present or talk about something about Hong Kong, it would be that although it is a large city, (and everyone is always nice to each other), it is a city of lights.

I would like to visit Kenya. My wishes are that one day I would be able to stand in that country and be able to communicate with the people, and be able to help.

EXTRA:

I Hope that will help with your book.

ISABIRYE (UGANDA)

- What is your name?

- Isabirye Michael Arthur.

- Your place of birth?

- Jinja, Uganda

- Are you living in your country of birth? And if not why did you choose to live where you are?

- Yes am living in my country of Birth.

- What are you and your closer friends frightened of, in the world?

- Aids, Terrorists and Being Poor.

- In one word, what is your wish for the world?

- Love

- Say a positive thing you like or you pay a little attention to, in the world!

- I would like to see love among all nations.

- If you would like to present or talk about something of positive about the culture of your country of birth or the town, the community where you are living, what it could be?

- The love and friendship that exists among my people and the ways through which the youths are getting rid of poverty.

- Tell us about a foreign country, that you have not visited yet, but which for a reason or other, comes in your mind sometimes or often. And what are your wishes for this country's population?

- One foreign Country I would like to visit is Ethiopia because of the peace that exists in this country, the people that live in this country and the culture that exists in this country.

S. DAVIS (USA)

- What is your name?

- S. Davis Slater.

- Your place of birth?

- Hyde Park, New York

- Are you living in your country of birth? And if not why did you choose to live where you are?

- Yes

- What are you and your closer friends frightened of, in the world?

- I am concerned with the economic inequalities in the world, and the over consumption of American's in the face of severe poverty in other countries.

- In one word, what is your wish for the world?

- Selflessness

- Say a positive thing you like or you pay a little attention to, in the world!

- All people have love in their hearts. They tie their hands in other ways, but in the end there is love and there is some desire to make things better.

- If you would like to present or talk about something of positive about the culture of your country of birth, the town, or the community where you are living, what could it be?

- There are public bathrooms everywhere you go.

- Tell us about a foreign country, that you have not visited yet, but which for a reason or other, comes in your mind sometimes or often. And what are your wishes for this country's population?

- I think of West Africa and how joyful there lives are in many ways, despite struggling.

MARY THERESE (PHILIPINE)

- What is your name?

- I am Mary Therese Nicole v. Isaac.

- Your place of birth?

- I was born on august 4, 1991, in Antipolo, Rizal, Philippines.

- Are you living in your country of birth? And if not why did you choose to live where you are?

- I am still living in my country of birth.

- What are you and your closer friends frightened of, in the world?

- Well I guess we're afraid to loose each other

- In one word, what is your wish for the world?

- Peace

- Say a positive thing you like or you pay a little attention to, in the world!

- Care for the environment

- If you would like to present or talk about something of positive about the culture of your country of birth, the town, or the community where you are living, what could it be?

- Too many things, I don't know what to say.

- Tell us about a foreign country, that you have not visited yet, but which for a reason or other, comes in your mind sometimes or often. And what are your wishes for this country's population?

- United states help!

CONCLUSION

I already said that some of those answers have surprised me, I hope that you have read them, and I am sure that they left you with some feelings. As I use to think about other culture, I knew that many people were doing the same thing, but the question was: What do they think? I just wanted to know if they have the same reflections I use to have. Now I have an answer to that question, some of them have similar opinions; some of them have different opinions regarding some points. But they all need peace for the world; most of them are frightened of war. They all have a foreign culture or people which they are thinking about, sometimes. Those words left me with something very special; now I have the feeling that the intercultural dialogue is more then possible.

Yes it is possible, to join different cultures, different groups. We just have to show love and respect to each other, to share and imagine how to do positive things together. Cultural exchange can favor the enlargement of the big garden of cultural diversity, and culture of peace around the world.

As I use to say: We have a lot to do, we have to work together, I think that none of us will success alone. It is so nice to admire that mixing of people from different cultures.

It is too nice to see their smile, their gesture... I invite you to do like me, let's think about the others. Let's ask: what do some Indian people are doing now? Let's say, how nice they are with their dot on the face. Let's think about South America, the mountains of Peru, the beaches of Brazil, Argentina, and Chile etc. What a nice music is the salsa...

Many people have returned me the same questions I asked, I think it would not be fair if I refused to answer. I'm sure that even you would like to know what I would answer; on the next page, you will have the opportunity to read my replies to my own questions. Before leaving, please let's say yes to the intercultural dialogue, cultural exchange, cultural diversity, mutual understanding, culture of peace and tolerance around the world.

MY ANSWERS:

My name is Francklin, I was born in Jérémie a little town located in the south part of

Haiti a small Republic, which shares with the Dominican Republic the island of Hispaniola, located in the Caribbean Sea, in front of the Gulf of Mexico. I am still living there.

I use to talk to some friends about that question of fear; we agree that we are frightened of war, incurable disease, to be destroyed like the dinosaurs.

I wish many positives thing to the world, but in one world my wish is: "Sharing".

What I really pay attention to nowadays is: the intercultural dialogue, the promotion of cultural exchange, cultural diversity, and creativity. I'm always looking for intercultural platform.

About my culture! Haiti, my country of birth has a very rich culture; many people all over the world know and agree that Haiti is culturally rich. Haitian paintings are very nice, famous and attractive. But I think that the Haitian hospitality is a great thing, and deserves that people talk about it.

To finish, I am going to repeat some words I use to say: "Always think about others" I use to think about many countries, it would be very difficult for me to mention all of them, but the Caribbean zone and the south of America often come in my mind, specially Chile, Costa-Rica, Equator, and Peru. I don't visit these countries yet, but I really feel something special for these people, their culture etc. I wish these countries in the south of America to continue to progress, and I would like that they never forget to take care of the originality of their culture.

To all of the countries of the Caribbean zone like Jamaica, Dominican Republic, and Trinidad and Tobago etc. I wish unity. I would like them to always remember that we are all West Indians.

To the Creole people, around the world, like from: Sainte Lucia, Dominica, Guadeloupe, Seashell island, Mauricio island, Reunion, Rodrigues island, etc. I wish and hope that they will join and work together for the progress and the promotion of the Creole culture. It's our job to promote our civilization and we will do it.

If you are interested in cultural exchange, cultural diversity, mutual understanding, join my blog: www.kiltiris.com

For Public comments go to the "About us" forum on kiltiris.com.

Send Private Comments to: *contact@francklin.com*

About us
propos de nous
cerca de nosotros

Francklin Pierre

ISBN 978-0-557-07808-0

A propos de nous

Un remerciement spécial

A tous ceux qui ont participé à la réalisation
de cette publication. Spécialement :

Francesca Palli (Suise)

Jean Yves et Michèle Trévien (France)

Paula Salomon (Argentine)

Je dédie cette ce projet à mon ancienne école de formation
humanitaire, le collège Roger A. Anglade

Et

A la mémoire de mon grand-père et de ma grand-mère :

Saint Louis Pierre et Osanna Lestin Pierre

INTRODUCTION

Comme d'habitude, j'étais là, en train de penser au dialogue
interculturel, quand j'ai eu l'idée de réaliser ce projet.
Comme d'habitude, j'étais là, en train de penser aux autres,
quand ce moment arriva   où

je me suis demandé: suis-je le seul en ce moment à penser à ces gens ? Suis-je le seul en ce moment à penser à d'autres cultures ? J'essayais de trouver quelques réponses, mais je me suis dit que finalement la meilleure façon était de poser ces questions aux autres et je me suis tout de suite mis au travail. J'ai imaginé huit petites questions qui permettraient à quelques personnes de dire qui elles sont, d'où elles sont, où se trouvent-elles, qu'est-ce qui les effraie, leur souhait pour ce monde, ce qu'elles aiment, à quoi elles prêtent leur attention, qu'est-ce qui est positif à propos de leur propre culture, à quels peuples étrangers il leur arrive de penser et pourquoi ? Les questions ont été lancées et j'étais très heureux quand j'ai commencé à recevoir quelques réponses. Comme je l'ai promis à ces gens qui ont participé, j'ai fait de mon mieux pour partager leurs mots avec le reste du monde. Certains ont répondu en anglais, d'autres l'ont fait en français et d'autres en espagnol. J'ai choisi, certaines réponses dans chacune des langues mentionnées ci-dessus étant toutes magnifiques, le choix était difficile.

Le dialogue interculturel est nous ; il peut seulement nous rendre plus fort. Nous pouvons beaucoup faire ensemble, c'est si intéressant de prendre soin et de penser aux autres. Chaque culture a quelque chose à dire. Disons oui au dialogue interculturel, à la culture de la paix et de la tolérance à travers le monde. S'il vous plaît, lisez ces propos à cœur ouvert. Ils vous apporteront beaucoup de plaisir et de profonds sentiments.

FRANCESCA (SUISSE)

Question (Q) : Quel est votre nom ?

Réponse (R) :   Francesca.

Q :Votre lieu de naissance ?

R : Gerra-Gambarogno, canton Tessin en Suisse.

Q : Vivez-vous dans votre pays natal ? Si non pourquoi avez-vous choisi de vivre là où vous êtes ?

R : Oui, dans un village en face de celui où je suis née, parce qu'ici c'est un très beau pays. En ce moment, je vois depuis ma fenêtre le lac et les montagnes sous le soleil. On ne peut pas désirer autre chose. Je me considère très fortunée.

Q : De quoi vous et vos amis les plus proches avez peur dans le monde ?

R : De l'égoïsme.

Q : En un mot, quel est votre souhait pour le monde ?

R : J'aimerais qu'on se considère tous comme des frères avec nos différences qui devraient nous enrichir et non pas être sources de divisions.

Q : Citez quelque chose que vous aimez ou qui attire le plus votre attention dans le monde?

R :J'aime la nature non contaminée, et les enfants qui te redonnent un sourire, peu importe qui tu es, jeune, vieux, noir, blanc...

Q : Si vous aviez à exprimer quelque chose de positif au sujet de la culture de votre pays, de votre ville ou de votre communauté, que diriez-vous ?

R : C'est peut-être le fait d'avoir une culture italienne, n'étant pas italienne.

Q : Y-a-t'il un pays que vous n'avez jamais visité, mais qui, pour une raison quelconque, vous vient parfois à l'esprit ? Et quels sont vos souhaits et pensées spéciales pour ses habitants ?

R : Maintenant c'est bien sûr Haïti. Le fait de m'en occuper tous les jours m'a liée très fortement au destin de ton pays. J'espère qu'Haïti pourra finalement avoir des dirigeants honnêtes, intelligents bien formés, capables de résoudre les problèmes les plus graves.

SOPHONIE MYRTIL (HAITI)

Q: Quel est votre nom ?

R : Sophonie Myrthil

Q : Votre lieu de naissance ?

R : Port-au-Prince, Haïti

Q : Vivez-vous dans votre pays natal ? Si non pourquoi avez-vous choisi de vivre là où vous êtes ?

R : Oui

Q : De quoi vous et vos amis les plus proches avez peur dans le monde ?

R : Du viol, du kidnapping, de tout ce qui est mauvais et ce qui se passe surtout dans notre pays etc.

Q : En un mot, quel est votre souhait pour le monde?

R : Changement. Un grand changement de mentalité, de foi etc.

Q : Citez quelque chose que vous aimez ou qui attire le plus votre attention dans le monde?

R : La lutte pour la paix

Q : Si vous aviez à exprimer quelque chose de positif au sujet de la culture de votre pays, de votre ville ou de votre communauté, que diriez-vous ?

R : J'adore la gentillesse des paysans haïtiens

Q : Y-a-t'il un pays que vous n'avez jamais visité, mais qui, pour une raison quelconque, vous vient parfois à l'esprit ? Et quels sont vos souhaits et pensées spéciales pour ses habitants ?

Q : Le Canada, la France, les Etats-Unis, etc.

MARIKA (SUISSE)

Q : Quel est votre nom?

R : Marika Bricchi

Q : Votre lieu de naissance?

R : Locarno, Suisse

Q : Vivez-vous dans votre pays natal ? Si non pourquoi avez-vous choisi de vivre là où vous êtes ?

R : oui

Q : De quoi vous et vos amis les plus proches avez peur dans le monde ?

R : la guerre, le climat de la terre qui change, la nature qui disparaît.

Q : En un mot, quel est votre souhait pour le monde?

R : que l'environnement redevienne ce qu'il était, pur, avec beaucoup d'arbres, sans gaz nocifs dans l'atmosphère... et que la paix revienne dans le monde

Q : Citez quelque chose que vous aimez ou qui attire le plus votre attention dans le monde?

R : J'aime surtout la nature, les animaux...

Q : Si vous aviez à exprimer quelque chose de positif au sujet de la culture de votre pays, de votre ville ou de votre communauté, que diriez-vous ?

R : Il y a un lac nettoyé et de plus Locarno est une petite ville. Il n'y a donc pas trop de trafic ni de chaos, ... C'est plutôt tranquille... Et, si je peux ajouter quelque chose : Locarno est une ville sûre.

Q :Y-a-t'il un pays que vous n'avez jamais visité, mais qui, pour une raison quelconque, vous vient parfois à l'esprit ? Et quels sont vos souhaits et pensées spéciales pour ses habitants ?

R : L'Australie, parce que j'ai vu des photos et des vidéos. Ce pays m'attire beaucoup! De ce pays avec des forêts si grandes, la mer, les dauphins, les montagnes... J'espère que ce peuple pourra continuer à garder un équilibre avec la terre et que ses traditions resteront dans le temps.

MAURIZIA (SUISSE)

Q : Quel est votre nom?

R : Maurizia

Q : Votre lieu de naissance?

R : Locarno, Suisse

Q : Vivez-vous dans votre pays natal ? Si non pourquoi avez-vous choisi de vivre là où vous êtes ?

R : Je vis à Cerentino (Tessin, Suisse), un petit pays de montagne situé en Vallemaggia mais pendant la semaine je vis à Locarno avec mes soeurs à cause de l'école...

Q : De quoi vous et vos amis les plus proches avez peur dans le monde ?

R : De voir des personnes abandonnées qui ont plus que quiconque besoin des autres. En d'autres mots, je crains la solitude, parce que dans ce monde il y a beaucoup trop d'égoïsme!

Q : En un mot, quel est votre souhait pour le monde ?

R : Je souhaite que les citoyens réalisent ce que pourrait être un monde meilleur, qu'ils ouvrent les yeux, regardent la réalité en face et changent de mentalité une fois par toute!

Q : Citez quelque chose que vous aimez ou qui attire le plus votre attention dans le monde ?

R : J'aime beaucoup penser à notre monde comme un mélange de peuples et de cultures, même si quelquefois c'est la cause principale des guerres, mais si chacun apprend à respecter les autres, probablement nous aurions un monde meilleur!

Q: Si vous aviez à exprimer quelque chose de positif au sujet de la culture de votre pays, de votre ville ou de votre communauté, que diriez-vous ?

R: J'aime mon pays natal parce que nous vivons en pleine nature! J'aime beaucoup aussi la Suisse parce que on a plusieurs cultures et langues, en outre nous avons aussi plusieurs différents paysages...

Q: Quel pays étranger que vous n'aviez jamais visité, mais qui pour une raison quelconque vous vient parfois à l'esprit. Et quels sont vos souhaits et pensées spéciales pour ce peuple?

R: un jour j'aimerai visiter l'Asie...j'aimerai voyager beaucoup, les pays que me viennent surtout à l'esprit sont le

Tibet, Népal, Nouvelle Zélande, Inde,...J'admire beaucoup leur culture, leur traditions et la simplicité de ces peuples...c'est magnifique comme ces gens n'ont presque rien mais sont si généreux et ils sourient toujours!

THEA FACCIO (SUISSE)

Q : Quel est votre nom?

R : Thea Faccio

Q : Votre lieu de naissance?

R: Minusio, Ticino, Svizzera

Q : Vivez-vous dans votre pays natal? Et si non pourquoi vous avez choisi de vivre là où vous êtes?

R : Oui, depuis je suis né.

Q : De quoi vous et vos amis les plus proches avez peur, dans le monde?

R : J'ai peur de la force et la puissance des effets de la mentalité de certaines personnes. (Ex. Bush)

Q : En un mot, quel est votre souhait pour le monde ?

 R : la paix et le savoir écouter et comprendre la parole des autres.

Q : Citez quelque chose que vous aimez ou qui attire le plus votre attention, dans le monde ?

R : la culture, la nature e les traditions des différents pays.

Q : Si vous aimeriez présenter ou parler de quelque chose de positif au sujet de la culture de votre pays natal ou de la ville, de la communauté où vous vivez, que pourrait-il être?

R : Nos traditions et surtout notre végétation.

Q : Quel pays étranger que vous n'avez jamais visité, mais qui pour une raison quelconque vous vient à l'esprit. Et quels sont vos souhaits et pensées spéciales pour ce peuple ?

R : Je voudrais aller en Argentine pour trouver mon oncle et pour découvrir un pays très loin par la distance mais très voisin avec le coeur.

VANJA (SUISSE)

Q : Quel est votre nom?

R : Vanja

Q : Votre lieu de naissance?

R : Tessin, Suisse

Q : Vivez-vous dans votre pays natal?

R : Oui

Q : De quoi vous et vos amis les plus proches avez peur, dans le monde ?

R : Guerre, désastre naturel (causé par l'homme)

Q : En un mot, quel est votre souhait pour le monde?

R : Félicité, joie

Q : Citez quelque chose que vous aimez ou qui attire le plus votre attention, dans le monde?

R : La nature

Q : Si vous aimeriez présenter ou parler de quelque chose de positif au sujet de la culture de votre pays natal ou de la ville, de la communauté où vous vivez, que pourrait-il être?

R : Nous suisses, sommes très fortunés: il y a la liberté, pas de guerre, la démocratie. Mais clairement la Suisse a aussi ses défections.

Q : Quel pays étranger que vous n'avez jamais visité, mais qui pour une raison quelconque vous vient parfois à l'esprit. Et quels sont vos souhaits et pensées spéciales pour ce peuple?

R : Suède, j'espère que ce pays continue d'être comme il est aujourd'hui, et avoir un bon respect pour la nature

SÊSSI (FRANCE)

J'ai eu la chance d'avoir des échanges directs avec certains des participants. Sêssi est l'une d'entre eux.

Q FRANCKLIN : Vous vous appelez comment?

 R SESSI : Sêssi

Q FRANCKLIN : Vous êtes née où ?

R SESSI : je suis née à Paris dans le onzième arrondissement

Q FRANCKLIN : Vivez-vous à Paris?

R SESSI : non pas actuellement, mais il y a quelques mois oui,

Q FRANCKLIN : Vous vivez où actuellement ?

R SESSI : dans une ville du 93, Montreuil, à Toronto, au Canada

Q FRANCKLIN : De quoi vous et vos amis les plus proches avez peur, dans le monde?

R SESSI : le plus peur? Du manque d'humanité, de la méchanceté gratuite, de l'extrême violence. Je ne peux parler à la place de mes amis, chaque être est unique. Ce qu'on peut ressentir face à un évènement varie d'un individu à l'autre.

Q FRANCKLIN : Entre amis vous n'en n'avez jamais parlé du manque d'humanité, ou disons, de ce dont vous avez peur le plus dans le monde.

R SESSI : De certains de ces hommes qui peuplent cette planète? Oui, d'ailleurs ça me rappelle mon sujet de baccalauréat en 1992 qui était : de philosophie: Pourquoi l'homme peut-il être si inhumain ? On en parle sous différentes formes, pas nécessairement comme je lai exprimé

Q FRANCKLIN : Vous avez peur du manque d'humanité c'est ça?

R SESSI : oui c'est ça, du manque d'humanisme de certains êtres humains qui vivent sur cette terre avec nous, qui nourrissent des sentiments de haine envers leurs propres frères ou leurs voisins.

Q FRANCKLIN : Vous avez un message ayant rapport au manque d'humanisme?

Q SESSI : j'ai un message sur quelque chose de plus positif que le manque d'humanisme.

Q FRANCKLIN : Donc vous refusez d'en parler?

R SESSI : non ce n'est pas ça mais je n'ai pas de message en tête par rapport à ça.

Q FRANCKLIN : Vous en avez peur ? Ça vous dérange ? Vous avez un souhait quand même?

R SESSI : oui j'en ai

Q FRANCKLIN : Quel est votre souhait à propos du manque d'humanité?

R SESSI : j'aimerais que chaque homme aie la possibilité de réaliser ses rêves et se donne aussi les moyens de les réaliser au sens le plus noble du terme. C'est à dire de ne pas tuer de ne pas voler, de ne pas torturer l'autre pour réaliser ses rêves de pouvoir ou de domination mais de pouvoir servir son prochain comme peut le faire pour soi- même. Jacques

Brel disait les hommes sont malheureux parce qu'ils ne réalisent pas les rêves qu'ils ont

Q FRANCKLIN : En un mot, quel est votre souhait pour le monde?

Q SESSI : Un monde digne de ce nom, plus humain, plus serein, que l'on préserve, que l'on aime et qu'on fait grandir vers le meilleur de ses potentialités ou comme le disait aussi Paul Valery: Mettons en commun ce que nous avons de meilleur et enrichissons nous de nos mutuelles différences. Un monde ou la diversité est synonyme de richesse et non de conflits de heurts.

Q FRANCKLIN : Vous avez parlé de Jacques Brel qui es-t-il?

R SESSI : Un chanteur français, un des plus illustres.

Q FRANCKLIN : Vous m'avez dit pas mal de choses concernant ton souhait pour le monde. Mais je reviens encore avec la question: Dites moi en un seul mot, quel est votre souhait pour le monde.

R SESSI : un mot : humanité

Q FRANCKLIN : Citez quelque chose que vous aimez ou qui attire le plus votre attention, dans le monde ?

R SESSI : découverte, voyage, culture.

Q FRANCKLIN : Si vous aimeriez présenter ou parler de quelque chose de positif au sujet de la culture de votre pays natal ou la ville, la communauté où vous vivez, que pourrait-il être ?

R SESSI : je suis béninoise d'origine, née à Paris, ayant grandi à Paris, voyageant a travers l'Afrique, l'Europe, l'Amérique du Nord ce qui a de plus positif dans ma culture d'origine c'est de constater que malgré tous les coups durs que nous avons reçu, et je ne parle pas seulement de mon pays mais de mon continent, preuve de notre grand sens de l'humour, le rire est purement culturel car c'est encré en chacun de nous.

Q FRANCKLIN : le sens de l'humour de votre peuple, c'est ça?

R SESSI : nous savons rire de nous même, j'élargirais au continent, que ça soit dans la danse dans les chants dans les créations artistique picturales nous pouvons retrouver cet aspect la qui me plait énormément nous pouvons rire de choses légères comme de choses graves.

Q FRANCKLIN : Quel pays étranger que vous n'aviez jamais visité, mais qui pour une raison quelconque vous vient parfois à l'esprit. Et quels sont vos souhaits et pensées spéciales pour ce peuple ?

R SESSI : il y en a beaucoup !

Q FRANCKLIN : d'accord mais, citez-en un

R SESSI : mais un spécial

Q FRANCKLIN : un seul !

R SESSI : l'Afrique du Sud, un pays qui a eu un passé historique très lourd

Q FRANCKLIN : Vous avez une pensée spécial pour ce peuple?

R SESSI : Que leur souffrances passées ou présentes soient leur force.

Q FRANCKLIN : Vous avez d'autres mots?

Q SESSI : J'ai déjà trop parlé!

Q FRANCKLIN : D'accord, (RIRE) Etant donné que vous m'aviez dit que vous en avez beaucoup ! Pour finir, pouvez-vous citer un autre pays qui vous vient à l'esprit ?

R SESSI : le Cambodge.

Q FRANCKLIN : Quel est votre souhait pour le peuple Cambodgien?

R SESSI : j'ai vu une émission télévisée, sur ce pays, et j'ai eu envie le visiter

Q FRANCKLIN : et quelle est la pensée pour eux?

R SESSI : je ne sais pas je ne connais pas bien l'histoire de ce pays, mais je sais que c'est un pays et un peuple avec des ressources historiques et naturelles fabuleuse, les temples d'Angkor.

Q FRANCKLIN : le souhait pour finir !

R SESSI : le temple j'aimerais le visiter, je n'ai pas de souhait spécifique pour ce pays je ne le connais qu'en images. Mais je l'aime bien !

Q FRANCKLIN : Merci, et je suis très heureux de vous avoir parler, merci encore.

Q SESSI : Pour le début, quand je parle de manque d'humanité pour les choses qui me font peur, tu peux aussi utiliser le mot BARBARIE pour résumer ma pensée. Merci à toi aussi.

TOIHIR IBRAHIM (COMORES)

Q : Quel est votre nom ?

R : Je me nomme Ibrahim MOHAMED TOIHIR

Q : votre lieu de naissance ?

R : je suis né évidemment dans un petit village, tout près de Moroni, la capitale des Comores, appelé TSIDJE.

Q : vivez-vous dans votre pays natal ? Et si non pourquoi vous avez choisi de vivre là où vous êtes ?

R : à défaut d'une université, à l'époque, répondant à ma filière dans mon pays natal, je me suis trouvé à Madagascar, île voisine et grande île de l'océan indien pour compléter mes études. Bref, je n'ai pas choisi de vivre ici mais juste le temps suffisant de pouvoir faire ma carrière universitaire. Ce n'est pas mal d'ajouter que le pouvoir d'achat malgache correspond bien à ma capacité économique. Tout cela par la forte dépréciation du franc malgache par rapport à l'Euro. En fait, un étudiant comorien issu de la couche sociale moyenne supporte bien les coûts d'études à Madagascar que dans tout autre pays du continent.

Q : De quoi vous et vos amis les plus proches avez peur, dans le monde ?

R : Moi particulièrement et je suppose être le cas de mes amis les plus proches, avons peur de la fin du monde. Que j'aimerais bien disparaître bien avant cette fin terrible! Car selon les livres sacrés, la fin du monde est un événement insupportable.

Q : En un mot, quel est votre souhait pour le monde ?

R : En un mot, je souhaite que ce monde se mette dans l'ordre comme ça l'était bien originellement. Je ne veux pas parler du point de vu évolutif mais vis-à-vis de la société.

Q : Citez quelque chose que vous aimez ou qui attire le plus votre attention, dans le monde?

R : En tant que naturaliste, tout ce qui attire mon attention ce sont les découvertes scientifiques et les nouvelles inventions dans tous les domaines.

Q : Si vous aimeriez présenter ou parler de quelque chose de positif au sujet de la culture de votre pays, de la ville, ou de la communauté où vous vivez, que pourrait-il être ?

R : Si je m'amuse à parler d'un point positif de ma culture ce serait l'hospitalité. Le comorien, d'où qu'il vienne, est hospitalier. Tout étranger, en arrivant aux Comores se sent chez lui. Malgré, des petits troubles politiques ces derniers temps, les Comores sont tout de même, en tête de l'île Maurice, le pays le plus accueillant de l'océan indien.

Q : Quel pays étranger que vous n'aviez jamais visité, mais qui pour une raison quelconque vous vient parfois à l'esprit. Et quels sont vos souhaits et pensées spéciales pour ce peuple ?

R : Le Canada est le pays étranger qui me fascine. D'abord, par son peuple fortement multicolore, il accueille tout ce qui lui tend la main. Dépourvu de racisme, et d'instabilité politique, loin d'être surpeuplé, le Canada est le pays industrialisé, selon moi, qui devrait servir de modèle. Comme leur devise le dit « d'un continent à l'autre », je souhaite que ce caractère généreux et anti-raciste du peuple canadien, reste éternel.

CONCLUSION

J'ai déjà dit que parmi les réponses reçues, plus d'une m'ont étonnées, j'espère que vous les avez lus, et je suis sûr qu'ils vous ont aussi laissé avec un sentiment quelconque... Tout comme j'ai l'habitude de penser à d'autres cultures, J'ai su ou pouvais imaginer que d'autres personnes font pareil, mais la question était: A quoi pensent-ils ? J'ai voulu justement savoir s'ils ont eu les mêmes impressions que moi.

Maintenant j'ai une réponse à cette question, je sais que certains d'entre eux ont une opinion assez proche de la mienne, d'autres sur certains points sont un peu différents. Mais ils ont tous besoin de paix dans le monde, la majorité d'entre eux sont effrayés par l'éventualité d'une guerre ou tout simplement par la « Guerre ». Ils ont une culture ou un peuple étranger auquel ils pensent parfois. Ces mots m'ont laissé avec quelque chose de très spécial, ils m'ont laissé avec l'impression que le dialogue interculturel est plus que possible. Il est bien possible, que des cultures ou groupes étrangers se joignent.

Nous devons nous aimer, partager des idées, et imaginer comment réaliser des choses positives ensemble. Le dialogue interculturel favorise l'épanouissement du grand jardin de la diversité culturelle et de la culture de paix à travers le monde. Nous avons beaucoup à faire, nous devons travailler ensemble, je pense qu'aucun de nous n'arrivera au succès en solitaire. Il est si agréable d'admirer le mélange des peuples, des cultures des quatre coins du monde. Il est si agréable d'admirer leurs sourires, leurs gestes... Je vous invite à faire comme moi, pensons aux autres. Demandons-nous ce que font les Indiens maintenant ? Pensons à l'Amérique du sud, aux montagnes du Pérou, aux plages du Brésil, d'Argentine, du Chili etc. Disons : Quelle belle musique est la salsa! Et la vieille Europe ! L'histoire et la littérature de France, L'art russe, La vie à Vienne…

Beaucoup de gens m'ont retourné les mêmes questions que j'ai posées, je pense qu'il serait injuste de ne pas leur répondre. Je suis sûr que, même vous, vous aimeriez savoir ce que je répondrais. A la page suivante, vous aurez l'occasion de lire mes réponses à mes propres questions. Avant de vous laisser, encore une fois, disons; oui au dialogue interculturel, à la promotion des échanges et la diversité culturelles, à la compréhension mutuelle. A la culture de la paix et la tolérance à travers le monde.

MES REPONSES

Q : Quel est votre nom ?

R : Mon nom est Francklin

Q : Votre lieu de naissance ?

R : je suis né à Jérémie une petite ville située dans la partie du sud d'Haïti une petite République, qui partage avec la République Dominicaine l'île d'Hispaniola, localisé dans la mer des Antilles, en face du Golfe du Mexique.

R : vivez-vous dans votre pays natal ? Et si non pourquoi vous avez choisi de vivre là où vous êtes ?

R : Je vis toujours en Haïti.

Q : De quoi vous et vos amis les plus proches avez peur, dans le monde ?

R : J'ai l'habitude de discuter avec quelques amis de cette question de crainte ; nous consentons que nous ayons peur de la guerre, des maladies incurables, d'être détruits comme les dinosaures.

Q : En un mot, quel est votre souhait pour le monde?

R : Je souhaite beaucoup de choses positives pour le monde, mais en un mot mon souhait est : Partage ! Je crois dans le partage.

Q : Citez quelque chose que vous aimez ou qui attire le plus votre attention, dans le monde ?

R : Ce à quoi je prête vraiment l'attention aujourd'hui est le dialogue interculturel, la diversité culturelle, je suis toujours à la recherche de plate-forme interculturelle.

Q : si vous aimeriez présenter ou parler de quelque chose de positive au sujet de la culture de votre pays natal ou la ville, la communauté où vous vivez, que pourrait-il être ?

R : Haïti, mon pays de naissance a une culture très riche, beaucoup de gens partout à travers le monde admettent qu'Haïti est culturellement riche. L'art haïtien, particulièrement les tableaux haïtiens sont magnifiques, célèbres et attrayants. Mais je pense que l'hospitalité haïtienne est aussi une grande chose, et mérite qu'on en parle.

Q : Quel pays étranger que vous n'aviez jamais visité, mais qui pour une raison quelconque vous vient parfois à l'esprit. Et quels sont vos souhaits et pensées spéciales pour ce peuple ?

R : Pour finir, je répéterai quelques mots que j'ai l'habitude de dire : « Pensons toujours aux autres » je pense souvent à beaucoup de pays, il est donc très difficile pour moi de les mentionner tous, mais la Caraïbe et l'Amérique du sud me viennent souvent en tête, spécialement des pays comme le Chili, le Costa Rica, l'Equateur et le Pérou. Pourtant, je n'ai pas encore visité ces pays, mais je sens vraiment quelque chose de spécial pour ces peuples, leur culture etc. Je souhaite que ces pays d'Amérique du sud continuent de progresser et j'aimerais qu'ils ne négligent jamais de prendre soin de l'originalité de leur culture. A tous les pays de la Caraïbe comme la Jamaïque, Trinité et Tobago, la République Dominicaine etc. je souhaite l'unité. J'aimerais qu'ils n'oublient jamais que nous sommes tous des Caraïbéens. Aux peuples créoles à travers le monde comme Sainte Lucie, la Dominique, la Guadeloupe, les île Seychelles, l'île Maurice, la Réunion, Rodrigue, etc. Je souhaite et espère qu'ils se joindront et travailleront ensemble pour le progrès et la promotion de la culture créole. C'est à nous de promouvoir notre civilisation et nous le ferons.

Si vous êtes intéressés aux échanges culturels, à la diversité culturelle, la compréhension mutuelle, rejoignez mon blogue sur: www.kiltiris.com

Postez vos commentaires publics dans le forum "About us" sur kiltiris.com

Envoyez vos commentaires privés à: contact@francklin.com

About us
propos de nous
cerca de nosotros

Francklin Pierre

ISBN 978-0-557-07808-0

Acerca de nosotros

Especial gracias a todas esas personas que participaron en la realización de esta publicación, en particular a:

Francesca Palli, (Suiza)

Jean-Yves y Michèle Trevien (Francia)

Paula Salomon (Argentina)

Dedico este proyecto al "Collège, Roger A. Anglade", mi instituto anterior de enseñanza secundaria.

Y a la memoria de mi gran padre y madre Saint Louis Pierre y Osanna Lestin

INTRODUCCION

Como de costumbre, yo estuve allí, pensando en el diálogo intercultural, cuando la idea de realizar este proyecto vino a mi mente. Como de costumbre, yo estuve allí, pensando en los otros, cuando ese momento llegó y empecé a preguntarme a mi mismo: ¿soy yo el único ahora pensando en esas personas? ¿Soy yo el único en este momento pensando en otra cultura? Trataba de encontrar algunas respuestas, pero finalmente me dije: la mejor manera de saber si las respuestas son correctas y verdaderas, es preguntándolas a otras personas. Y empecé a trabajar inmediatamente sobre eso, imaginé ocho preguntas que darían lugar, a algunas personas, a decir: quiénes son, dónde están, de dónde son, a qué le temen, cuál es su deseo para el Mundo, qué es lo que adoran y a qué se dedican, qué es lo positivo de su propia cultura ¿En qué pueblo extranjero sueles pensar y por qué? Hice mis preguntas, y fui muy feliz al recibir algunas respuestas. Y como lo prometí a dichas personas que participaron, di lo mejor de mí para compartir sus palabras con el resto del mundo. Algunos de ellos respondieron en inglés, algunos lo hicieron en francés y otros en español, yo escogí con mucha dificultad algunos de ellos en cada uno los idiomas, todos fueron realmente agradables.

Sólo el diálogo intercultural puede fortalecernos, nosotros somos ese diálogo. Es tanto lo que podemos hacer juntos, y es tan bueno interesarse y pensar en el otro.

Cada cultura tiene mucho por decir. Digamos sí al diálogo intercultural, a la cultura de la paz y de la tolerancia en todo el mundo. Lee, por favor, estas opiniones con el corazón abierto. Leerlos alimentará tu alma y comprenderás más el mundo desde otras miradas.

SARA (SUIZA)

- ¿Cuál es tu nombre?

- Sara Fuentes Mezquita

- ¿Tu lugar de nacimiento?

- Locarno (Ticino, Suiza)

- ¿Vives en tu tierra natal? De no ser así, ¿por qué has decidido vivir dónde vives?

- Vivo en mi ciudad natal

- ¿A qué le temen tú y tus amigos más cercanos?

- A las catástrofes naturales

- ¿En una palabra, cuál es tu deseo para el mundo?

- Que todos vivan en tranquilidad. Que no haya injusticias y que todos puedan alimentarse y tener asistencia médica...

- ¿Qué es lo que más te interesa y aprecias en el mundo?

- La amistad que poseo con mis seres allegados.

- ¿Cuál crees que es el aspecto más favorable de la cultura de tu tierra natal, de la ciudad o comunidad donde vives?

- Es una nación segura, no hay mucha pobreza y es políticamente segura.

- ¿Has pensado en algún país que nunca hayas visitado? ¿Cuáles serían tus expresiones de deseo para éste?

- California es un país que me gustaría visitar, no creo que tenga muchos problemas políticos, no estoy muy informada, pero me gustaría que no haya nunca una guerra o cualquiera otra injusticia.

EXTRA

Le deseo mucha suerte para su próximo libro... Un saludo desde Suiza

JOSE (HONDURAS)

- ¿Cuál es tu nombre?

- José Roberto Solís Mayén

- ¿Tu lugar de nacimiento?

- Tegucigalpa Honduras

- ¿Vives en tu tierra natal? De no ser así, ¿por qué has decidido vivir dónde vives?

- Si

- ¿A qué le temen tú y tus amigos más cercanos?

- Terrorismo, intolerancia, falta de oportunidades

- ¿En una palabra, cuál es tu deseo para el mundo?

- Paz

- ¿Qué es lo que más te interesa y aprecias en el mundo?

- Personas, niñez, la cultura, diversidad.

- ¿Cuál crees que es el aspecto más favorable de la cultura de tu tierra natal, de la ciudad o comunidad donde vives?

- En realidad siento que la cultura de mi país es casi inexistente. Hay una gran falta de identidad cultural, por lo que me será casi imposible resaltar algo bueno.

- ¿Has pensado en algún país que nunca hayas visitado? ¿Cuáles serían tus expresiones de deseo para éste?

- Italia. La cuna del arte en mi parecer, uno de los únicos países que ha logrado conservar ese misterio y encanto ancestral después de tanto tiempo. La gente es cálida y amable, me parece que sería un sueño ir allí.

EXTRA

Me complace saber que existen personas que se interesen por la diversidad cultural, por lo que es un placer ayudarte en tu proyecto.

MELIDA PATRICIA (SALVADOR)

- ¿Cuál es tu nombre?

- Mélida Patricia Chereguino González.

- ¿Tu lugar de nacimiento?

- San Salvador, El Salvador.

- ¿Vives en tu tierra natal? De no ser así, ¿por qué has decidido vivir dónde vives?

- Sí vivo en la capital de El Salvador.

- ¿A qué le temen tú y tus amigos más cercanos?

- De la violencia y de la corrupción. De la falta de empleo y oportunidades.

- ¿En una palabra, cuál es su deseo para el mundo?

- Amor

- ¿Qué es lo que más te interesa y aprecias en el mundo?

- La sonrisa sincera de mi gente.

- ¿Cuál crees que es el aspecto más favorable de la cultura de tu tierra natal, de la ciudad o comunidad donde vives?

- La gente misma, su implacable lucha por superarse y salir adelante.

- ¿Has pensado en algún país que nunca hayas visitado? ¿Cuáles serían tus expresiones de deseo para éste?

- México, les deseo justicia y paz.

MARIANA KATY (NUEVA ZELANDIA)

- ¿Cuál es tu nombre?

- Mi nombre es Mariana Katy Stone GLEDHILL (tengo solamente 1 apellido)

- ¿Su lugar de nacimiento?

- Nueva Zelanda

- ¿Vives en tu tierra natal? De no ser así, ¿por qué has decidido vivir dónde vives?

- No, sino vivo en Perú. Estoy trabajando acá por seis meses, con niños de la calle

- ¿A qué le temen tú y tus amigos más cercanos?

- Yo, ahora.... perros.... no estoy bromeando.... los cambios en el ambiente en el mundo y las cosas que los estados unidos quieren hacer...y políticos que hacen cosas estúpidas.... también las diferencias entre pobres y ricos. Y mi amiga tiene cáncer. Tengo miedo que ella vaya a morir. Guerra, violencia...

- ¿En una palabra, cuál es su deseo para el mundo?

- Sobrevivir

- ¿Qué es lo que más te interesa y aprecias en el mundo?

- Mi familia y amigos

- ¿Cuál crees que es el aspecto más favorable de la cultura de tu tierra natal, de la ciudad o comunidad donde vives?

- Las personas en mi país no luchan mucho. Cuando hay manifestaciones, no hay violencia.... (Nueva Zelanda)

- ¿Has pensado en algún país que nunca hayas visitado? ¿Cuáles serían tus expresiones de deseo para éste?

- La India... parece que la gente allá es muy interesante y tienen muchas costumbres diferentes a las mías. Tengo mucho interés. No sé porque...

JOSE ARCHIMBAUD (PERU)

- ¿Cuál es tu nombre?

- Mi nombre es Jose Archimbaud.

- ¿Tu lugar de nacimiento?

- Lima Perú.

- ¿Vives en tu tierra natal? De no ser así, ¿por qué has decidido vivir dónde vives?

- Si

- ¿A qué le temen tú y tus amigos más cercanos?

- A la globalización y a las guerras por el poder Económico de las grandes potencias y de la poca voluntad que tienen estas para ayudar a que los países tercermundistas logren nivelarse económicamente.

- ¿En una palabra, cuál es su deseo para el mundo?

- Estoy conciente de que la problemática mundial es muy compleja pero yo desearía que cada persona ponga algo de su parte para ayudar a vivir en un mundo mas justo y mas solidario no somos concientes ni siquiera de que nosotros mismos nos estamos destruyendo.

- ¿Qué es lo que más te interesa y aprecias en el mundo?

- Me gusta la acción que realiza la gente de defensa del medio ambiente interesado en mantener el equilibrio de la vida salvaje en el mundo.

- ¿Cuál crees que es el aspecto más favorable de la cultura de tu tierra natal, de la ciudad o comunidad donde vives?

- Bueno nuestra cultura es rica en anécdotas variadas pero lo principal es el legado que nos dejaron nuestros antiguos pobladores del Perú manteniendo un equilibrio y armonía con los animales y la tierra su modos de vida eran simples muy agradecidos con la Mama Pacha la madre tierra creo que ahora hay muy poca gente que se interesa por algo así.

- ¿Has pensado en algún país que nunca hayas visitado? ¿Cuáles serían tus expresiones de deseo para éste?

- El "Tibet", me imagino a la gente muy religiosa y agradecida con quien ellos piensan son sus creadores, sus Dioses. Si me gustaría tener

mas personas para participar he intercambiar ideas.

CONCLUSION

Yo ya he dicho que algunas de estas respuestas me han sorprendido, espero que tú las hayas leído, y sé que te han dejado sensaciones, también. Como yo tengo la costumbre de pensar en otra cultura, muchas otras personas hacen lo mismo, pero la pregunta fue: ¿Qué piensan ellos? Ahora tengo una repuesta a esa pregunta, algunos de ellos tienen una opinión más cercana a la mía, algunos de ellos en cierto punto tienen difieren. Pero todos necesitan la paz para el mundo, la mayoría de ellos le temen a la guerra. Todos tienen una cultura o país extranjero en los que piensan a veces.

Esas palabras me dejaron con algo muy especial, ellos me dejaron con el sentimiento de que el diálogo intercultural es más que posible. Sí es posible, para unir culturas diferentes, grupos diferentes. Tenemos que adorarnos unos a otros, compartir y imaginar cómo hacer cosas positivas juntas. El diálogo intercultural puede favorecer el desarrollo del gran jardín de la diversidad cultural, y de la cultura de la paz alrededor del mundo. Usualmente digo: Tenemos mucho por hacer, tenemos que trabajar juntos, yo pienso que ninguno de nosotros puede crecer sólo. Es tan fascinante la mezcla de pueblos de culturas diferentes. Es tan agradable ver su sonrisa, su gesto... Los invito a ustedes a hacer como yo, pensar en los otros. ¿Preguntemos: qué hacen algunas personas de India ahora? Digamos, que contentos ellos están con su punto en la cara. Pensemos en América del Sur, en las montañas de Perú, en las playas de Brasil, de Argentina, de Chile etc. Qué música agradable es la salsa...

Muchas personas me han hecho las mismas preguntas que pregunté, pienso que no contestar no seria justo. Yo se que aún usted querría saber lo que contestaría; debajo, usted tendrá la oportunidad de leer mis respuestas a mis propias preguntas. Antes de terminar, una vez mas, por favor digamos sí al diálogo intercultural, a la cultura de la paz y de la tolerancia alrededor del mundo.

MIS REPUESTAS:

FRANCKLIN (HAITI)

Me llamo Francklin, nací en Jérémie, una pequeña ciudad localizada en la parte sur de Haití una pequeña República, que comparte con la República Dominicana la isla de Hispañola, localizada en el Mar del caribe, a la entrada del Golfo de México. Vivo todavía allí.

Usualmente yo hablo a algunos amigos del objeto de temor; concordamos que nos asusta la guerra, la enfermedad incurable, y tememos ser destruidos como los dinosaurios.

Deseo muchas cosas positivas para el mundo, pero en una palabra mi deseo es: *Compartir*.

¿Qué atiende realmente a, hoy? El diálogo intercultural, la diversidad cultural, yo siempre busco a plataforma intercultural.

Ahora acerca de mi cultura. Haití, mi país de nacimiento tiene una cultura muy rica, muchas personas por todo el mundo saben y concuerdan que Haití es culturalmente rico. Las pinturas haitianas son muy agradables, famosas y atractivas. Pero pienso que la hospitalidad haitiana es una grande cosa, y merece ser nombrada.

Para terminar, repetiré algunas palabras que digo usualmente: "Yo siempre pienso en otro" pienso usualmente en muchos países, es muy difícil para mí de mencionarlos todos, pero el caribe y América del sur a menudo entran en mi mente, especialmente Chile, Costa Rica, el Ecuador, Perú... No he visitado esos países aún, pero siento realmente algo especial con sus pueblos, su cultura etc. Deseo que esos países en América del Sur continúen progresando, y quisiera que nunca olviden preservar su cultura, lo original de ella. A todos los países del caribe como Jamaica, República Dominicana, Trinidad y Tobago, deseo la unidad. Querría que ellos nunca se olviden que somos todos antillanos. A los pueblos criollos de todo el mundo como: Santa Lucía, Dominica, Guadalupe, la isla de "Seyshell", Islas Mauricio, la Reunión, Isla Rodrigues, etc. Deseo y confío en que se unirán y trabajarán juntos para el progreso y la promoción de la cultura criolla. Es nuestro trabajo promover nuestra civilización y lo haremos.

¡Aprecie este trabajo a su manera!

Si estás interesando en intercambio cultural, diversidad cultural, comprensión mutual, ven a mi bog: www.kiltiris.com

Para los comentarios públicos, va al foro "About us" en kiltiris.com

Comentarios privados a: <u>*contact@francklin.com*</u>